So You Want to Be President?

BY Judith St. George

ILLUSTRATED BY David Small

PHILOMEL BOOKS

There are good things about being President and there are bad things about being President. One of the good things is that the President lives in a big white house called the White House.

Another good thing about being President is that the President has a swimming pool, bowling alley, and movie theater.

The President never has to take out the garbage.

The President doesn't have to eat yucky vegetables. As a boy, George Bush had to eat broccoli. When George Bush grew up, he became President. That was the end of the broccoli!

One of the bad things about being President is that the President always has to be dressed up. William McKinley wore a frock coat, vest, pin-striped trousers, stiff white shirt, black satin tie, gloves, a top hat, and a red carnation in his buttonhole every day!

The President has to be polite to everyone. The President can't go anywhere alone. The President has lots of homework.

McKINLEY

People get mad at the President. Someone once threw a cabbage at William Howard Taft. That didn't bother Taft. He quipped, "I see that one of my adversaries has lost his head."

Lots of people want to be President. If you want to be President, it might help if your name is James. Six Presidents were named James. (President Carter liked to be called Jimmy). Four Johns, four Williams (President Clinton liked to be called Bill), two Georges, two Andrews, and two Franklins—all became President.

James Madison

William Harrison

William McKinley

William Taft

William Clinton

John Adams

Andrew Jackson

Andrew Johnson

James Monroe

James Polk

James Buchanan

James Garfield

James Carter

CALL ME JIMMY

John Quincy Adams

GEORGE

George Washington

John Tyler

George Bush

John Kennedy

JOHN

Franklin Pierce

Franklin Roosevelt

FRANKLIN

Zachary Taylor

James Polk

Andrew Jackson

Millard Fillmore

You probably weren't born in a log cabin. That's too bad. People are crazy about log-cabin Presidents. They elected eight. William Harrison was born in a big Virginia mansion, though he won the election with a "log cabin and hard cider" slogan.

If you want to be President, your size doesn't matter. Presidents have come in all shapes and sizes. Abraham Lincoln was the tallest—six feet four inches. (His stovepipe hat made him look even taller.)

James Madison was the smallest—five feet four inches and only one hundred pounds. William Howard Taft was the biggest—more than three hundred pounds. He was so big that he had a special tub built for his White House bathroom. (Four men could fit in the tub!)

Maybe Taft's problem was that Presidents can order any food they want. Andrew Johnson once served his guests turtle soup, oysters, fish, beef, turkey, mutton chops, chicken, mushrooms, string beans, partridges, duck, pudding, jellies, and lots of wine. All at one dinner!

Though the Constitution says you'll have to wait until you're thirty-five, young, old, and in between have become President. Theodore (Teddy) Roosevelt at forty-two was the youngest. He had pillow fights with his children and played football on the White House lawn. "You must always remember that the President is about six," a friend said. Ronald Reagan was the oldest. When he first ran for President, he was sixty-nine. He joked that it was the thirtieth anniversary of his thirty-ninth birthday.

Some Presidents joked and some didn't—Presidents' personalities have all been different. William McKinley was so nice that he tried to stop a mob from attacking the man who had just shot him. Benjamin Harrison was so cold that one senator said talking to Harrison was like talking to a hitching post. Calvin Coolidge was so shy and quiet that a dinner guest once made a bet that she could get him to say more than two words. "You lose," he told her. Andrew Jackson certainly wasn't shy. When he ran for President, his opponents printed a list of his duels, fights, shootings, and brawls. Fourteen in all!

Don't worry about your looks. Abraham Lincoln was a homely man, but he was one of our best Presidents. (He reunited the country by winning the Civil War.) Someone once called Lincoln two-faced. "If I am two-faced, would I wear the face that I have now?" Lincoln asked.

Warren Harding was a handsome man,
but he was one of our worst Presidents. (He gave
government jobs to his crooked friends.) "I am not fit for this
office and never should have been here," he admitted.

Do you have pesky brothers and sisters? Every one of our Presidents did. Benjamin Harrison takes the prize—he had eleven! (It's lucky he grew up on a six-hundred-acre farm.) James Polk and James Buchanan both had nine. George Washington, Thomas Jefferson, James Madison, and John Kennedy each had eight.
(Two Presidents were orphans, Andrew Jackson and Herbert Hoover.)

A President in your family tree is a plus. John Quincy Adams was John Adams' son. Theodore Roosevelt and Franklin Roosevelt were fifth cousins. Benjamin Harrison was William Harrison's grandson. James Madison and Zachary Taylor were second cousins.

Some Presidents threw money around and some were penny pinchers. James Monroe ordered French silverware, china, candlesticks, chandeliers, clocks, mirrors, vases, rugs, draperies, and furniture for the White House. Ninety-three crates in all!

William Harrison was thrifty. He walked to market every morning with a basket over his arm.

Do you have a pet? All kinds of pets have lived in the White House, mostly dogs. Herbert Hoover had three dogs: Piney, Snowflake, and Tut. (Tut must have been a Democrat. He and his Republican master never got along.) Franklin Roosevelt's dog, Fala, was almost as famous as his owner.

George Bush's dog wrote MILLIE'S BOOK: ADVENTURES OF A WHITE HOUSE DOG (as reported to Mrs. Bush!). Ulysses Grant had horses, Benjamin Harrison's goat pulled his grandchildren around in a cart, the Coolidges had a pet raccoon, Jimmy Carter and Bill Clinton preferred cats.

Theodore Roosevelt's children didn't just have pets, they ran a zoo.
They had dogs, cats, guinea pigs, snakes, mice, rats, badgers,
raccoons, parrots, and a Shetland pony called Algonquin. To cheer
up his sick brother, young Quentin once took Algonquin upstairs
in the White House elevator!

You don't have to be musical to be President. Ulysses Grant certainly wasn't. He knew only two tunes. "One is 'Yankee Doodle'," he said, "and the other one isn't."

But many Presidents were musical. Thomas Jefferson, John Tyler, and Woodrow Wilson played the violin; John Quincy Adams, the flute; Chester Arthur, the banjo; Harry Truman and Richard Nixon, the piano; Bill Clinton, the saxophone, and Warren Harding almost any brass instrument, including the sousaphone.

Some Presidents knew how to dance and some didn't. Our first President did a mean minuet. At his inaugural ball George Washington danced with every lady but his wife. (Mrs. W. had stayed home!) James Madison's opinion of his inaugural ball? "I would much rather be in bed." Abraham Lincoln wasn't much of a dancer. "Miss Todd, I should like to dance with you the worst way," he told his future wife. Miss Todd later said to a friend, "He certainly did." Woodrow Wilson liked to do the jig step while singing silly ditties.

Not all Presidents danced, but most had a sport. John Quincy
Adams was a first-rate swimmer. Once when he was skinny-dipping in
the Potomac River, a woman reporter snatched his clothes and sat on
them until he gave her an interview.

Ulysses Grant raced his rig through the streets of Washington (and was arrested for speeding!). Rutherford Hayes played croquet on the White House lawn. Ronald Reagan split wood. William McKinley's idea of exercise was to sit under a tree with a good book.

Golf has been big with Presidents. Dwight Eisenhower and John Kennedy were especially good. But when Gerald Ford, George Bush, and Bill Clinton teamed up for a golf game, three of their shots clobbered spectators!

Though most Presidents went to college, nine didn't: George Washington, Andrew Jackson, Martin Van Buren, Zachary Taylor, Millard Fillmore, Abraham Lincoln, Andrew Johnson, Grover Cleveland, and Harry Truman. (Andrew Johnson couldn't read until he was fourteen! He didn't learn to write until after he was married!)

Thomas Jefferson was top-notch in the brains department—he was an expert on agriculture, law, politics, music, geography, surveying, philosophy, and botany. In his spare time he designed his own house (a mansion), founded the University of Virginia, and whipped up the Declaration of Independence.

If you want to be President, you might consider joining the army. George Washington, Andrew Jackson, William Harrison, Zachary Taylor, Ulysses Grant, Rutherford Hayes, James Garfield, Chester Arthur, Benjamin Harrison, and Dwight Eisenhower were all generals.

If you can't be a general, be a hero like Theodore Roosevelt or John Kennedy. (Roosevelt's Rough Riders charged up Kettle Hill to help win the Spanish-American War. Kennedy led his crew to safety in World War II when the Japanese sank his PT boat.)

Don't be a Franklin Pierce. In his very first battle, Franklin Pierce's horse bucked, he was thrown against his saddle and fainted, his horse fell, broke its leg, and Pierce hurt his knee. (He got elected anyway!)

Another route to the White House is to be Vice President, though most don't think much of the job. Truman's Vice President, Alben Barkley, told about a man who had two sons. One son went to sea, the other was elected Vice President. Neither was ever heard from again. (Who's ever heard of Alben Barkley?)

Other Vice Presidents have been heard from. John Adams, Thomas Jefferson, Martin Van Buren, Richard Nixon, and George Bush were all elected President. (Gerald Ford became President when Richard Nixon resigned.) John Tyler, Millard Fillmore, Calvin Coolidge, and Harry Truman moved up when a President got sick and died. Andrew Johnson, Chester Arthur, Theodore Roosevelt, and Lyndon Johnson became top man when guns were drawn, bullets flew, and a President was assassinated!

Almost any job can lead to the White House. Presidents have been lawyers, teachers, farmers, sailors, engineers, surveyors, mayors, governors, congressmen, senators, and ambassadors. (Harry Truman owned a men's shop. Andrew Johnson was a tailor. Ronald Reagan was a movie actor!)

One thing is certain, if you want to be President—and stay President—be honest. Harry Truman paid for his own postage stamps. Grover Cleveland was famous for his motto: "Tell the truth."

Other Presidents weren't so honest. Democrat Bill Clinton was impeached for lying under oath. Republican Richard Nixon's staff broke into Democratic headquarters to steal campaign secrets. He covered up the crime and then lied about it. (That was the end of Richard Nixon as President!)

There they are, a mixed bag of forty-one Presidents! What did they think of being head man? George Washington, who became our very first President in 1789, worried about his new line of work. "I greatly fear that my countrymen will expect too much from me," he wrote to a friend. (He was a howling success.) Some loved the job. "No President has ever enjoyed himself as much as I," Theodore Roosevelt said. Others hated it. "The four most miserable years of my life," John Quincy Adams complained.

Every President was different from
every other and yet no woman has been
President. No person of color has been President.
No person who wasn't a Protestant or a Roman
Catholic has been President. But if you care enough, anything
is possible. Thirty-four Presidents came and went before a Roman
Catholic—John Kennedy—was elected. Almost two hundred years
passed before a woman—Geraldine Ferraro—ran for Vice President.

It's said that people who run for President have swelled heads. It's said that people who run for President are greedy. They want power. They want fame.

But being President can be wanting to serve your country—like George Washington, who left the Virginia plantation he loved three times to lead the country he loved even more.

It can be looking toward the future like Thomas Jefferson, who bought the Louisiana Territory and then sent Lewis and Clark west to find a route to the Pacific. (They did!)

It can be wanting to turn lives around like Franklin Roosevelt, who provided soup and bread for the hungry, jobs for the jobless, and funds for the elderly to live on.

It can be wanting to make the world a better place like John Kennedy, who sent Peace Corps volunteers around the globe to teach and help others.

Every single President has taken this oath: "I do solemnly swear (or affirm) that I will faithfully execute the office of President of the United States, and will to the best of my ability, preserve, protect, and defend the Constitution of the United States."

Only thirty-five words! But it's a big order when you're President of this country. Abraham Lincoln was tops at filling that order. "I know very well that many others might in this matter as in others, do better than I can," he said. "But . . . I am here. I must do the best I can, and bear the responsibility of taking the course which I feel I ought to take."

That's the bottom line. Tall, short, fat, thin, talkative, quiet, vain, humble, lawyer, teacher, or soldier—this is what most of our Presidents have tried to do, each in his own way. Some succeeded. Some failed. If you want to be President—a good President—pattern yourself after the best. Our best have asked more of themselves than they thought they could give. They have had the courage, spirit, and will to do what they knew was right. Most of all, their first priority has always been the people and the country they served.

Featured in Illustrations

left to right unless otherwise noted

1. **George Washington** (1789-1797)—Born Westmoreland County, Virginia, 1732—Died 1799. As first President of the United States, Revolutionary War hero George Washington put his permanent stamp on the presidency.

2. **John Adams** (1797-1801)—Born Braintree, Massachusetts, 1735—Died 1826. John Adams, who was the first President to live in the White House, saved the country from fighting a needless war with France.

3. **Thomas Jefferson** (1801-1809)—Born Goochland County, Virginia, 1743—Died 1826. A man of wide learning, Thomas Jefferson bought the Louisiana Territory, which doubled the size of the United States.

4. **James Madison** (1809-1817)—Born Port Conway, Virginia, 1751—Died 1836. While Madison was President during the War of 1812, the British set fire to the White House.

5. **James Monroe** (1817-1825)—Born Westmoreland County, Virginia, 1758—Died 1831. James Monroe's Monroe Doctrine, which warned European powers to stay out of the Americas, has stood the test of time.

6. **John Quincy Adams** (1825-1829)—Born Braintree, Massachusetts, 1767—Died 1848. John Adams' son, John Quincy Adams served his government brilliantly for over forty years, but accomplished little as President.

7. **Andrew Jackson** (1829-1837)—Born The Waxhaws, South Carolina, 1767—Died 1845. Elected by the "common man," Andrew Jackson greatly expanded the powers of the presidency.

8. **Martin Van Buren** (1837-1841)—Born Kinderhook, New York, 1782—Died 1862. Martin Van Buren's policies deepened a severe economic depression.

9. **William H. Harrison** (1841)—Born Charles City County, Virginia, 1773—Died 1841. A military hero of the western frontier, William Harrison died after only a month in office.

10. **John Tyler** (1841-1845)—Born Charles City County, Virginia, 1790—Died 1862. John Tyler, who set a precedent by becoming President rather than Acting President after Harrison's death, annexed Texas.

11. **James K. Polk** (1845-1849)—Born Mecklenburg County, North Carolina, 1795—Died 1849. During Polk's administration, the United States gained 525,000 square miles of western territory by winning the Mexican War.

12. **Zachary Taylor** (1849-1850)—Born Orange County, Virginia, 1784—Died 1850. Zachary Taylor, who took a strong stand on preserving the Union, died after sixteen months in office.

13. **Millard Fillmore** (1850-1853)—Born Locke, New York, 1800—Died 1874. Millard Fillmore supported the Compromise of 1850, which offended both the North and the slave-holding South.

14. **Franklin Pierce** (1853-1857)—Born Hillsboro, New Hampshire, 1804—Died 1869. Tensions over slavery increased during Franklin Pierce's presidency, especially in "Bleeding Kansas," where armed conflict broke out.

15. **James Buchanan** (1857-1861)—Born Cove Gap, Pennsylvania, 1791—Died 1868. The only bachelor President, James Buchanan witnessed seven Southern states secede from the Union.

16. **Abraham Lincoln** (1861-1865)—Born Hardin County, Kentucky, 1809—Died 1865. Before his assassination, Abraham Lincoln sustained the North through the Civil War, ended slavery, and reunited the country.

17. **Andrew Johnson** (1865-1869)—Born Raleigh, North Carolina, 1808—Died 1875. Andrew Johnson, who bought Alaska from Russia, was acquitted of impeachment charges by a single Senate vote.

18. **Ulysses S. Grant** (1869-1877)—Born Point Pleasant, Ohio, 1822—Died 1885. Although Ulysses Grant was known to be honest personally, his administration was tarnished by scandal.

19. **Rutherford B. Hayes** (1877-1881)—Born Delaware, Ohio, 1822—Died 1893. Rutherford Hayes became President after the country's most fiercely debated election.

20. **James A. Garfield** (1881)—Born Orange Township, Ohio, 1831—Died 1881.

James Garfield, who was shot after only four months in office, died two months later.

21. **Chester A. Arthur** (1881-1885)—Born Fairfield, Vermont, 1830—Died 1886. Chester Arthur reformed the civil service system and approved the beginnings of the modern American Navy.

22. and 24. **Grover Cleveland** (1885-1889 and 1893-1897)—Born Caldwell, New Jersey, 1837—Died 1908. Grover Cleveland was the only President to serve two non-consecutive terms.

23. **Benjamin Harrison** (1889-1893)—Born North Bend, Ohio, 1833—Died 1901. Benjamin Harrison, who was William Harrison's grandson, allowed party leaders to run the country.

25. **William McKinley** (1897-1901)—Born Niles, Ohio, 1843—Died 1901. William McKinley was assassinated after the United States acquired overseas territory by winning the Spanish-American War.

26. **Theodore Roosevelt** (1901-1909)—Born in New York, New York, 1858—Died 1919. Under Theodore Roosevelt the United States became a world power while new laws at home bettered American lives.

27. **William H. Taft** (1909-1913)—Born Cincinnati, Ohio, 1857—Died 1930. Taft was the only President who later served as Chief Justice of the Supreme Court.

28. **Woodrow Wilson** (1913-1921)—Born Staunton, Virginia, 1856—Died 1924. After the Allied victory in World War I, Woodrow Wilson lost his health while trying to gain support for the League of Nations.

29. **Warren G. Harding** (1921-1923)—Born Blooming Grove, Ohio, 1865—Died 1923. Warren Harding, who appointed dishonest friends to government office, died before the scandal broke.

30. **Calvin Coolidge** (1923-1929)—Born Plymouth Notch, Vermont, 1872—Died 1933. Although Calvin Coolidge restored honesty to the White House, social and economic problems worsened.

31. **Herbert C. Hoover** (1929-1933)—Born West Branch, Iowa, 1874—Died 1964. Herbert Hoover, who headed up food relief for famine-stricken Europe after both World Wars, was President when the country's worst economic depression began.

32. **Franklin D. Roosevelt** (1933-1945)—Born Hyde Park, New York, 1882—Died 1945. Elected for four terms that spanned the Great Depression and World War II, Franklin Roosevelt made sweeping social changes before dying in office.

33. **Harry S. Truman** (1945-1953)—Born Lamar, Missouri, 1884—Died 1972. The atomic bomb, World War II victory, the Cold War, the Truman Doctrine, and the Korean War highlighted Harry Truman's presidency.

34. **Dwight D. Eisenhower** (1953-1961)—Born Denison, Texas, 1890—Died 1969. "Ike" ended the Korean War and kept the peace despite intense Communist pressures.

35. **John F. Kennedy** (1961-1963)—Born Brookline, Massachusetts, 1917—Died 1963. Only forty-three when he was elected, John Kennedy, who founded the Peace Corps, was assassinated before he could prove himself.

36. **Lyndon B. Johnson** (1963-1969)—Born Stonewall, Texas, 1908—Died 1973. Although Lyndon Johnson masterminded social reforms, the country was torn apart by his escalation of the Vietnam War.

37. **Richard M. Nixon** (1969-1974)—Born Yorba Linda, California, 1913—Died 1994. Richard Nixon ended the Vietnam War and opened talks with Communist China but resigned over his illegal role in the Watergate break-in.

38. **Gerald R. Ford** (1974-1977)—Born Omaha, Nebraska, 1913— The only chief executive never elected either Vice President or President, Gerald Ford pardoned Richard Nixon.

39. **James E. Carter, Jr.** (1977-1981)—Born Plains, Georgia, 1924— Although he was politically inexperienced, Jimmy Carter supervised the Israel-Egypt peace treaty.

40. **Ronald W. Reagan** (1981-1989)—Born Tampico, Illinois, 1911—The oldest President ever elected, Ronald Reagan, who was known as the Great Communicator, launched the largest peacetime military buildup in American history.

41. **George H. W. Bush** (1989-1993)—Born Milton, Massachusetts, 1924—The main concerns of George Bush's presidency were the Gulf War and the collapse of Soviet Communism.

42. **William J. Clinton** (1993-)—Born Hope, Arkansas, 1946—Bill Clinton, whose presidency focused on social issues, was impeached by the House of Representatives, but acquitted by the Senate.

For Peter—J.St.G.

To Sarah—D.S.

BIBLIOGRAPHY

Athearn, Robert G. **The American Heritage New Illustrated History of the United States.** Volumes 1-16. New York: Dell Publishing Co., Inc., 1963.

Freidel, Frank. **Our Country's Presidents.** Washington, D.C.: National Geographic Society, 1966.

Jensen, Oliver, ed. "The Presidency," **American Heritage**, Volume XV, Number 5 (August 1964). Special edition. New York: American Heritage Publishing Co., Inc.

Leish, Kenneth W., ed. **The American Heritage Book of the Presidents and Famous Americans**, Vols. 1-12, New York: American Heritage Publishing Co., Inc., 1967.

Seale, William. **The President's House: A History.** Volumes I, II. Washington, D.C.: White House Historical Association, 1986.

Taylor, Tim. **The Book of the Presidents**. New York: Arno Press, 1975.

Philomel Books would like to thank
Ross K. Baker,
Professor of Political Science at Rutgers University,
for his kind help.

Patricia Lee Gauch, editor

PHILOMEL BOOKS
a division of Penguin Putnam Books for Young Readers,
345 Hudson Street, New York, NY 10014.
Philomel Books, Reg. U.S. Pat. & Tm. Off. Published simultaneously in Canada.
Printed in the United States of America. The text is set in Golden Type ITC.
The art is done in ink, watercolor, and pastel chalk
Library of Congress Cataloging-in-Publication Data
St. George, Judith, So you want to be president? / by Judith St. George ; illustrated by David Small. p. cm.
Summary: Presents an assortment of facts about the qualifications and characteristics of U. S. presidents, from George
Washington to Bill Clinton. 1. Presidents—United States—Miscellanea—Juvenile literature. [Presidents—
Miscellanea.] I. Small, David, 1945- ill. II. Title. E176.1.S699 2000 973'.099—dc21 98-40002 CIP AC
ISBN 0-399-23407-1
3 5 7 9 10 8 6 4 2